Heartlake City
Adventures

LONDON, NEW YORK, MUNICH,
MELBOURNE, and DELHI

Senior Editors Tori Kosara, Helen Murray,
Lisa Stock
Designer Lauren Rosier
Jacket & Slipcase Designer Mark Penfound
Project Manager Sarah Harland
Design Manager Ron Stobbart
Art Director Lisa Lanzarini
Publishing Manager Julie Ferris
Publishing Director Simon Beecroft
DTP Designer Kavita Varma
Senior Producer Lloyd Robertson
Reading Consultant Dr. Linda Gambrell

This edition published in 2014
First published in the United States in 2012
by DK Publishing
345 Hudson Street
New York, New York 10014
A Penguin Random House Company

001—276097—Aug/14

LEGO, the LEGO logo, the Brick and Knob
configurations are trademarks of the LEGO Group.
© 2014 The LEGO Group.
Produced by Dorling Kindersley
under license from the LEGO Group.

Published in Great Britain by
Dorling Kindersley Limited.

A catalog record for this book is available
from the Library of Congress.

ISBN: 978-1-4654-3418-0

Color reproduction by Media Development and Printing, UK
Printed and bound in China by Leo Paper Products Ltd.

Discover more at
www.dk.com
www.LEGO.com

Contents

Heartlake City
Adventures

Friends Forever

Written by Helen Murray

A new home

Heartlake City is a wonderful place to live. Whether you love nature, relaxation, shopping, or going to cool parties and events, you are sure to find lots to do in this beautiful city. For one lucky girl, Heartlake City has just become her new home. Her name is Olivia and she is looking forward to all the fun and excitement the city promises.

Olivia can't wait to plan an outdoor adventure in the mountains, take a boat out onto Lake Heart, and go to open-air concerts in the park. But, most of all, Olivia is excited to make lots of new friends. With all the cool things to do in her new city, that should be no problem at all!

There are many different types of beautiful buildings in Heartlake City.

Olivia

Olivia has just moved to Heartlake City with her parents and their white cat, Missy.

Olivia is a clever, hardworking student and she is looking forward to studying at Heartlake School. Her favorite subjects are science, art, and history. Olivia is a practical person who loves to solve problems.

Olivia is always prepared. She carries a few useful tools in her pretty bag!

Missy
Olivia's cat, Missy, is very mischievous. She likes her new home because there are lots of good hiding places to discover!

She likes to make and fix things. One day she hopes to be a scientist, inventor, or engineer.

Olivia enjoys nature and hiking and she is eager to explore the beautiful woods, coastline, and mountains of Heartlake City. Unfortunately, this will have to wait because Olivia's parents have told her that she must unpack all of the boxes in her room first!

Olivia's family moved to Heartlake City because her dad, Peter, got a job as editor of the Heartlake Times. Olivia's mom, Anna, is a doctor.

She also has a new job, at Heartlake City hospital. Anna is a very kind and caring doctor.

Although Olivia's parents both work very hard, they always make time for their daughter. They go for family walks and bike rides, watch movies together, and sometimes help Olivia with her homework—although clever Olivia rarely needs any help!

Olivia's dad is a good listener. Olivia enjoys chatting to him while he tends to his vegetable garden in their new front yard.

A quiet place
Olivia loves her new swing. It has become her favorite place to think or write in her diary.

Olivia lives at Number 30, Heartlake Heights. It is a beautiful, big house with many rooms, including a large kitchen, a cozy family room, and Olivia's bedroom. The house has a huge front yard with a white picket fence, a vegetable garden, and pretty flowers. Olivia's favorite flowers are the pink ones that grow below her bedroom window because they attract beautiful butterflies.

Swing

Grill

There is also a rooftop terrace for sunbathing. Olivia's mom has put up an umbrella—just in case it gets too hot! Olivia's dad likes to cook outside. He has set up the big grill in the yard.

Rooftop terrace

Vegetable garden

·30·

Mailbox

Lawn mower

New friends

It has been two months since Olivia moved to Heartlake City. She loves her new town. There is always something fun and exciting happening here! But by far the best thing about her new home is her four fabulous friends.

Olivia   Emma   Stephanie   Andrea

It didn't take Olivia long to meet four of the coolest, smartest, and nicest girls in town—Andrea, Mia, Emma, and Stephanie. The five girls are now the best of friends.

The girls have even formed a Friends Club. They use their many skills and talents to solve all sorts of problems that arise in the city. Whether they are helping to find a runaway horse, fixing a collapsed stage, or planning a cool event in Heartlake City, the girls always have fun. Do you want to meet Olivia's new best friends?

Mia

Andrea

Andrea is the drama queen of the group. She loves to sing, dance, and act, and she often puts on performances for her friends. She dreams of one day becoming a superstar.

Andrea is very musical. Even her clothes have musical notes on them!

Andrea loves to perform on a floodlit stage for all of the city to hear.

Although Andrea is a wonderful dancer and actor, her real passion is music. She sings anywhere and everywhere. She sings on stage, at school, at the café where she works, and sometimes even in the shower!

Andrea will soon be the biggest star in Heartlake City. But Andrea does not plan to stop there—she has set her sights on a world tour.

Even budding superstars can have part-time jobs. Andrea works in the girls' favorite hangout, the City Park Café. She works with Marie, the owner, to make delicious milkshakes, cupcakes, pies, and hamburgers.

Hungry work
Andrea's favorite part of the job is testing the tasty new recipes. This burger and pink cupcake get her approval!

Andrea's tasks also include washing the dishes and sweeping the floor. But even at work, Andrea dreams of stardom. She can often be found singing into the broom handle instead of sweeping or serving customers. Unfortunately for Andrea, the hungry customers are usually more interested in the food than her performance. Andrea's daydreams can also cause her to mix up the orders!

Just across the lake from the City Park Café, Andrea regularly performs at an open-air stage for all of Heartlake City to hear.

Andrea sings in the spotlight under a sign with her name on it—a sign that her talented friend Emma made. But Andrea hopes to one day see her name in lights, on a much bigger stage.

Stereo

Piano

Andrea is a talented composer and piano player as well as a singer. She writes and plays all her own songs.

Andrea is an amazing singer. She always brings the audience to their feet and receives a standing ovation. But nobody cheers as loudly as Emma, Olivia, Stephanie, and Mia!

Spotlight

Microphone

Light

Stage

Emma

Emma is an artist. She loves drawing, fashion, and interior design. She is talented but also very practical. Emma can turn anything she finds into something stylish and beautiful.

Her friends often tell Emma that she is forgetful, but she disagrees. After all, she would never forget to leave the house without accessorizing her outfit!

Emma has a magnificent white horse called Robin. They enter show jumping competitions together across Heartlake City. They practice hard and often win prizes. Of course, even Robin's stable is beautifully furnished—Emma likes to decorate the walls with colorful ribbons.

Emma takes photos of her designs to show her friends. The girls love to see her amazing creations.

Emma's biggest passion is fashion and she has a design studio packed with everything she needs to become the next big fashion designer.

Chest of drawers

Inspiration board

Laptop

Fabric

Lamp

Camera

Tape measure

Design table

Hard at work
Emma uses her laptop to research new ideas and to keep up to date with the latest fashion trends and runway shows.

She works at a large design table where she cuts out materials and sews clothes. She stores fabric, paper, and tools in the large pink and purple chest of drawers. Naturally, everything is color-coordinated in her studio! Emma is always looking for inspiration in Heartlake City. She takes her camera everywhere with her. She puts photos and drawings on the large inspiration board in her studio.

Emma uses her talents to give her friends amazing makeovers. Emma, Andrea, Stephanie, Mia, and Olivia love to go shopping together to find new clothes and accessories and to try out new looks. Their favorite boutique is Butterfly Beauty Shop on Main Street.

Puppy makeover
Emma has found the perfect look for Mia's puppy, Charlie. He is bound to win the Cutest Puppy award at Heartlake City's annual dog show.

The girls shop for barrettes, bows, sunglasses, and other cool accessories. Emma always knows what will look best. Her friends wait for the moment when she says "That's so you!"

Emma sometimes gets a little carried away with giving makeovers. Once she has finished creating new looks for the girls, she likes to give their pets makeovers, too! Luckily, the animals love being pampered.

Mia

Mia is crazy about animals. From mice to horses, and even bugs, Mia loves them all! She works part-time at Heartlake Vet with Olivia's Aunt Sophie. One day, Mia would like to become a vet or an animal trainer.

Mia owns a beautiful pony called Bella and an excitable spotty puppy named Charlie. But she also takes in many stray and injured animals and looks after them in her bedroom.

Mia works hard at Heartlake Vet. She is caring and practical. She would make a great vet!

Mia cares for the animals until they are better or she can find them a loving, new home.

Outdoor girl Mia loves to go camping, canoeing, and horseback riding, of course. She is learning to play the drums too, but she makes sure that there are no animals around when she practices. She doesn't want to scare them or hurt their ears!

Mia's favorite animal is her horse, Bella. She visits Bella in her stable every morning and evening. Mia makes sure that Bella has enough water and food, as well as clean straw to sleep on. Bella needs plenty of exercise, so Mia practices jumping with her, or goes for long rides in the woods. They spend so much time together that Emma sometimes accuses Mia of smelling of horses!

Bella has won countless ribbons and cups for show jumping.

Mia is a talented horseback rider. She enters show jumping competitions and often wins first place. Bella can jump incredibly high! Mia's biggest and oldest rival is Lacy and her horse, Gingersnap. Lacy is very competitive and loves to beat Mia. Although Mia likes to win, she knows that there are more important things in life than winning—such as being a good sport. And her best friends, of course!

Mia has a gift for looking after and training animals. She talks to the animals and they seem to be able to understand her! Animals always bond very quickly with Mia, so this makes training them much easier.

Tasty treat
Mia rewards clever Charlie with a bone for his hard work at the Heartlake City Dog Show.

Mia is training her puppy, Charlie. He is usually very well-behaved, but he does like to run through puddles! He is mostly white, so he gets dirty very quickly. Mia puts him in a tub and cleans him with a brush and special dog shampoo.

Charlie is young and he is still learning new tricks, but he has already mastered the obstacle course at Heartlake City's annual dog show. He has won two awards to prove it!

Stephanie

Stephanie is a born party planner. She loves to organize spectacular events, sleepovers, and adventures with the girls. Stephanie is a great friend to have around—she always gets the girls into the party spirit.

Stephanie can be a little bossy at times, but her friends know that it is just because she wants everything to go perfectly.

However, if anything ever does go wrong, Stephanie takes charge. She knows exactly what to do—and which of her friends should do it!

Stephanie has recently started taking flying lessons at the local flight school. If you see a plane overhead, it might just be her!

Stephanie's dog
Stephanie has a brown puppy called Coco. She makes sure that Coco always looks immaculate!

Stephanie believes that a party is not a party unless there is cake! She is an excellent baker and her cupcakes, birthday cakes, brownies, and pies always look perfect and taste wonderful. Stephanie is far too careful to let anything go wrong.

Umbrella

Cake

Brownie

Milk

Oven

Super-organized Stephanie never forgets her friends' birthdays and always bakes a cake for them.

Stephanie even has an outdoor bakery, which is perfect for garden parties—her favorite type of party. Here, Stephanie has just put the finishing touches to her party preparations. She has set up the outdoor table and umbrella and is waiting for her friends to arrive.

Stephanie carefully pours the cake ingredients into a large bowl. After thoroughly mixing, she pops it into her outdoor oven.

Stephanie loves to explore Heartlake City in her stylish purple and blue convertible. She loads her puppy Coco into the back and picks up her friends for the ride.

The girls drive to their favorite hangouts—the beach, the beauty shop, or the café. But Stephanie likes to plan more challenging adventures, too.

Grooming equipment

Windshield

MP3 player

Dog grooming basket

Stephanie fills up the bucket from the street faucet and adds car shampoo. She is ready to scrub!

The friends take road trips along the coast, to the forest, and even as far as the Clearspring Mountains at the edge of Heartlake City.

Stephanie is very proud of her car and likes to keep it clean and sparkling. She even manages to make washing her car fun! She listens to party tunes on her MP3 player and dances while she scrubs. Sometimes she washes Coco at the same time, too!

Secret hangout

Ssh! Don't tell anyone, but this is the secret headquarters of the Friends Club! Olivia found the treehouse on the day she moved to Heartlake City, and it is very close to her house. When she met Stephanie, Mia, Andrea, and Emma, she knew the treehouse would be the perfect hangout for the girls.

Practical Olivia and Emma both checked that the treehouse was safe, and all the friends worked together to create a beautiful girls-only space. They even fixed the cool folding ladder, which they lift up to stop anyone else from sneaking into their treehouse.

Bench

Lookout

Telescope

Folding ladder

Secret box

The girls like to camp out in their treehouse. Stephanie brings cupcakes for a midnight feast, and the friends share their secrets, hopes, and dreams under the beautiful night sky. The club telescope comes in handy to check that nobody is listening nearby!

Far and away
The girls can see Lake Heart, the ocean, and the Clearspring Mountains through the club telescope.

No secret club headquarters would be complete without a special hiding place. The girls keep their most treasured possessions inside a blue box. It is hidden at the base of the treehouse underneath tree branches. The friends love to search for treasure. One day, they hope to uncover Dark-Eyed Kate's pirate treasure on Lighthouse Island.

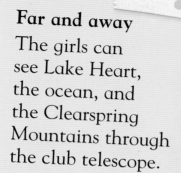

The treehouse can also be used as a temporary animal hospital. One day, Olivia and her friends found a poor yellow bird with a broken wing in their new treehouse headquarters. They named him Goldie and worked hard to nurse him back to health. The girls even built a red and white stripy birdhouse, which sits under the tree. Goldie liked his new home so much that he has stayed!

The girls worked together to build a bed for Maxie and a birdhouse for Goldie.

Olivia also found a stray cat, Maxie. She has become the club headquarters' resident cat. Andrea brings leftover fish and milk from the café as treats for Maxie. The little kitten likes to join the girls at their sleepovers, so they have made a cute little bed for Maxie to sleep in.

Friends forever

A lot has changed in Olivia's life over the past few months. She has moved to an amazing new town and made four wonderful best friends. Life is pretty great! Olivia, Emma, Andrea, Stephanie, and Mia have so much fun together and they always look out for each other. Olivia feels like she has known her four new friends forever, and can't wait to have many more adventures with them. She is sure that they will always be best friends.

Olivia's diary
Olivia has so much to write about! Her diary is packed with tales of her new friends and their adventures.

Summer Adventures

Written by Catherine Saunders

Summer's here!

It's summertime in Heartlake City. With no school for a few weeks, Mia, Olivia, Stephanie, Andrea, and Emma can enjoy the sunshine. Each girl has some great ideas for summer fun.

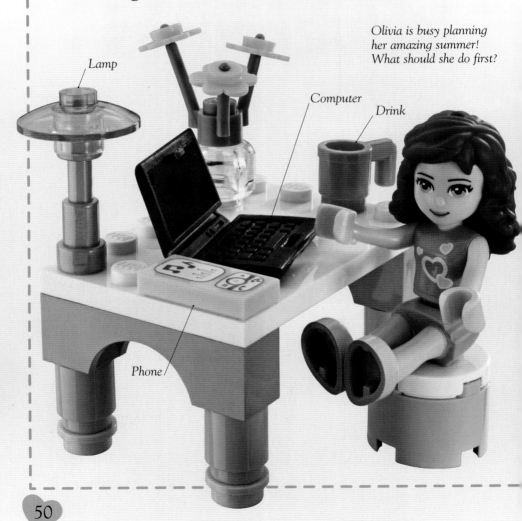

Olivia is busy planning her amazing summer! What should she do first?

Lamp

Computer

Drink

Phone

Andrea, Stephanie, Emma, Mia, and Olivia are looking forward to their summer vacations. They've all got some very exciting adventures planned.

Turn the page to find out who will be making sweet music, who is planning a trip, and who will be working hard. Discover who is off to riding camp, who will be taking to the skies, and, most importantly, what the girls will be doing together.

There's something exciting to suit everyone, so come and join the girls on their fantastic summer adventures.

Up, up, and away!

Stephanie thinks the best place to have a summer adventure is in the sky. She has a special type of plane that can take off and land on water. It's called a seaplane. Stephanie has been taking flying lessons at the Heartlake Flying Club for a few months. She's a natural!

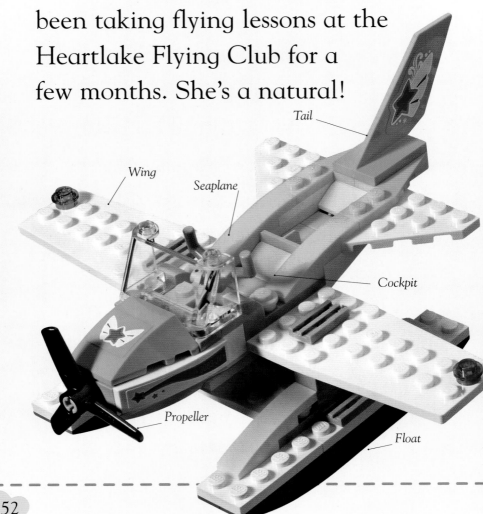

Tail

Wing

Seaplane

Cockpit

Propeller

Float

Stephanie is the newest—and youngest—member of the Heartlake City Flying Club.

At last, Stephanie is qualified to fly her seaplane all by herself. However, before she can set off on an exciting flying adventure, she must do some important safety checks. First she must check the weather forecast—flying in bad weather would not be fun. Next, she must plan her route and make sure she has enough fuel for the journey. Finally, Stephanie is ready for take off!

After a smooth take off, Stephanie is up, up, and away! The weather is perfect and Stephanie can see for miles. She is going to fly all around Heartlake City and see what her friends are doing.

Look! There's Mia. She's at the stables grooming her horse Bella. Is that Emma over there?

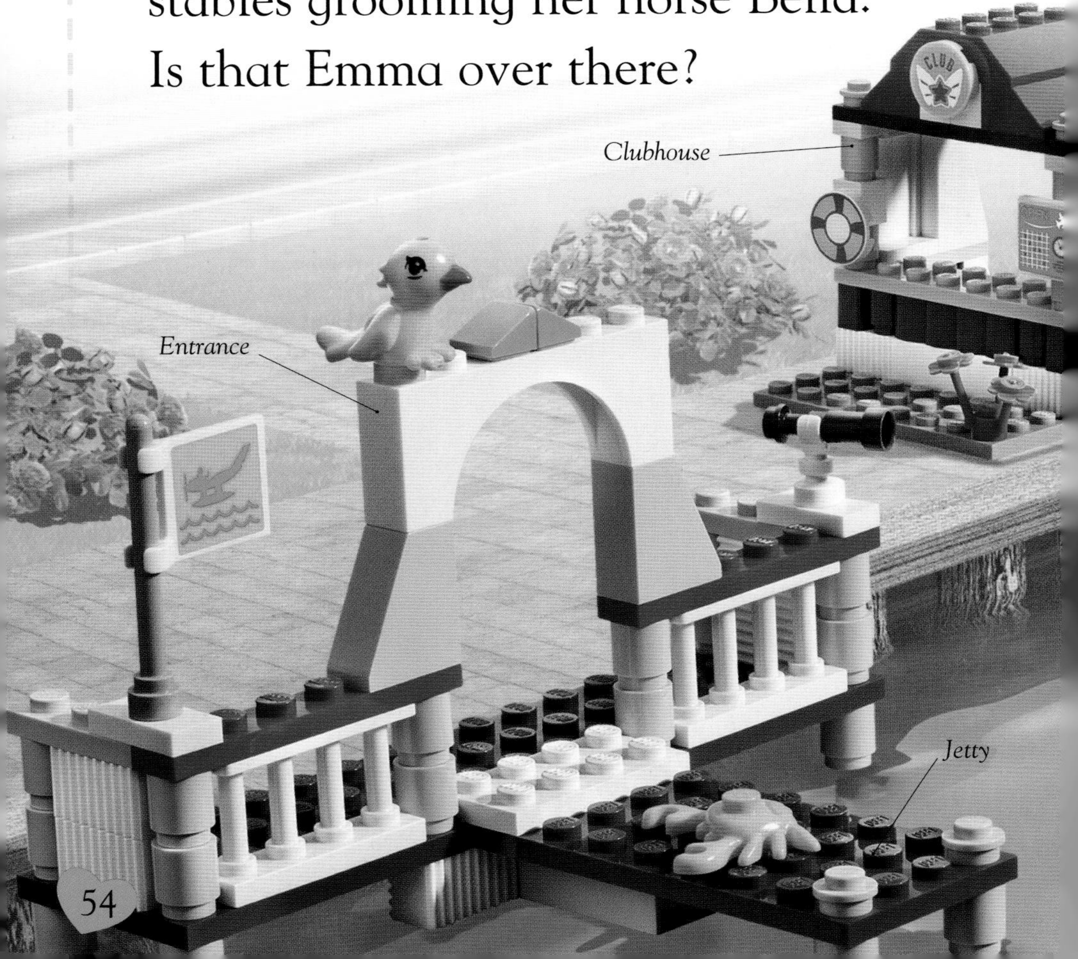

Clubhouse

Entrance

Jetty

Yes, she's shopping on Main Street. Now Stephanie is flying over Olivia's house; Olivia is building something amazing in the backyard. Stephanie knows just where to find Andrea: There she is, hard at work in the City Park Café. What a great trip! Now it's time for Stephanie to head back and make the perfect landing.

Map

Lights

Take a trip

Olivia thinks summer is the perfect time to take a trip in her camper van. She loves to explore the countryside around Heartlake City in the stylish pink van. It has a TV in the back and enough space for two people to sleep in it. Olivia knows just who she wants to share this summer adventure with—her friend, Nicole.

Camper van

Gal pals

Olivia and Nicole used to live in the same town, before Olivia moved to Heartlake City. They are good friends and meet up as often as they can.

Olivia calls Nicole and tells her about her plan. Nicole thinks it sounds like fun! The two girls pack their bags and load their bikes and surfboards into the trailer. It's time to set off on their summer adventure!

Bike

Surfboard

Trailer

Olivia has found a quiet spot to park the camper van, so the two friends set off on a bike ride. It's good exercise, and a great way to catch up. The two girls talk about everything that has happened since they last saw each other. Nicole has a new pet cat and has been taking cooking lessons.

Nicole

Olivia

Juice

Nicole is a very good cook. Grilled chicken is her specialty and Olivia can't wait to try it!

Olivia tells Nicole about her new friends Mia, Stephanie, Andrea, and Emma. Nicole thinks they sound like a lot of fun and would like to meet them all one day.

Back at their camp site, Olivia and Nicole are hungry after a long bike ride. While Olivia prepares a salad, Nicole cooks some chicken on the grill. What a great day!

After a great night's sleep in the camper van, Olivia and Nicole are ready for the next part of their adventure. Olivia drives them to the beach. The girls prepare a delicious picnic and then head down to the ocean with their surfboards.

Picnic
basket

The camper van has all the comforts of home, including a TV. It means that the girls won't miss their favorite shows while they're away.

The surf's up and the girls are ready to catch some waves. Nicole has never been surfing before, so Olivia shows her how to do it. After a few wipeouts, Nicole is an expert surfer.

The girls feel quite tired after a day of surfing so they decide to spend the evening relaxing in the van. They play games and watch TV. Tomorrow they will head back home. It's been a wonderful summer adventure!

Surfboard

Find the beat

Mia wants to learn a new skill this summer, so she is teaching herself how to play the drums. She has a cool set of drums and plans to play them every day in her bedroom.

Lamp

Drumstick

Sheet music

Personalized drums

Music fans

Andrea is a music fan, too. She likes to spend her time writing songs and practicing for her next concert.

Radio

Mia likes to practice by turning the radio up high and keeping the beat to her favorite songs. She's getting pretty good at it and is thinking about starting her own rock group. Her new hobby is very cool, but very, very loud. Mia's parents are pleased that she is interested in music, but they prefer her to practice when they're out!

Summer job

For Andrea, the summer is about working hard and saving money for the future. She works as a waitress at the City Park Café. She takes orders from the customers and then serves them delicious cakes and refreshing drinks. It's hard work, but Andrea doesn't mind because she's saving up for extra singing lessons.

Mia

Emma

After a hard day at work, Andrea is ready to relax and rest her tired feet. And she knows the perfect way to chill out—by sharing a milkshake with her friends at the City Park Café!

Emma and Mia join Andrea for a milkshake and a slice of one of Marie's famous pies.

Writing adventures

Stephanie is very sociable and she has many friends all over the world. It's a lot of work keeping in touch with all of them, but if anyone can do it, it's super-organized Stephanie! She loves to write long letters to her pen pals.

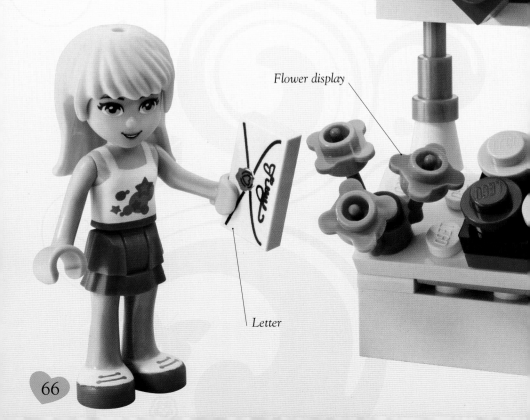

Flower display

Letter

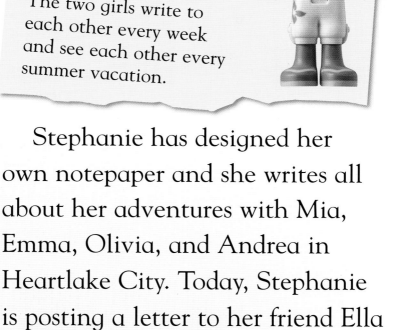

Pen pal

One of Stephanie's best pen friends is Ella. The two girls write to each other every week and see each other every summer vacation.

Stephanie has designed her own notepaper and she writes all about her adventures with Mia, Emma, Olivia, and Andrea in Heartlake City. Today, Stephanie is posting a letter to her friend Ella asking her if she wants to come to riding camp with Emma and her this summer.

Letterbox

Beach time

When she isn't working at the City Park Café or practicing her singing, Andrea heads to the beach. There's always something fabulous to do there!

Sandcastle

Crab

Flippers

If Andrea wants to take it easy, she can just relax and read her favorite book. But if she's looking for adventures, she can go snorkeling and discover the amazing ocean world or search for exciting treasure buried beneath the sandy beach.

Andrea also loves building sandcastles. Her friend Olivia has been teaching her how to construct the most spectacular castles, featuring towers, a moat, and a flag on top. Of course, no matter how well Andrea builds them, her pretty creations are always washed away by the ocean!

Time to relax

Emma thinks that summer isn't all about having exciting adventures. She likes to relax and take it easy after working so hard at school.

Her friends agree and they like to make time to just chill out together.

Sun umbrella

Olivia

Emma

Ice cream sundae

Sun lounger

Emma also has a splash pool in her backyard. It's perfect for taking a dip on a hot summer day.

Emma's summer house is right by the beach. It's the perfect place for Emma, Mia, Stephanie, Olivia, and Andrea to hang out, sunbathe, and catch up on each other's summer adventures. Relaxing in the sun can give the girls a healthy appetite, but they have the perfect snack—ice cream sundaes. They're cool, creamy, and completely delicious!

Outdoor adventures

Mia and Olivia agree that summer is no time to be stuck inside all the time. The weather is always good in Heartlake City so they both like to have exciting outdoor adventures.

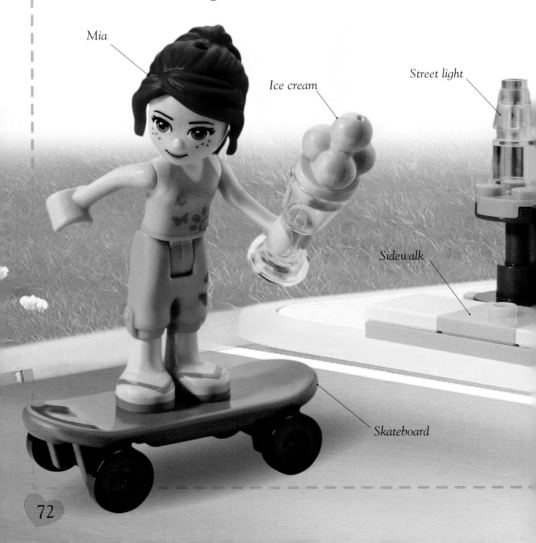

Mia

Ice cream

Street light

Sidewalk

Skateboard

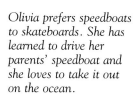

Olivia prefers speedboats to skateboards. She has learned to drive her parents' speedboat and she loves to take it out on the ocean.

Mia's favorite outdoor pastime is skateboarding. She spends a lot of time at the City Park practicing jumps and tricks. Soon she thinks she'll be ready to enter a local skateboarding competition. Skateboarding is also a great way of getting around—it's much quicker than walking! In fact, Mia is so good at skateboarding that she can skate and eat an ice cream at the same time. It's not as easy as it looks!

Indoor adventures

During the summer, Emma tries to spend as much time as possible in her studio. She wants to be a fashion designer so she's already working on her own fashion collection.

Snack

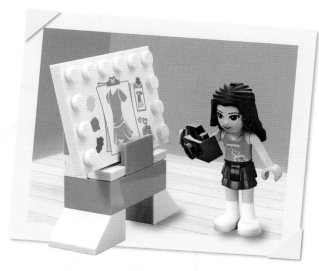

Emma thinks her latest creation would look fabulous on Mia!

Laptop

Emma has so many great ideas! In her studio, she uses the internet to research styles and fabrics, then she draws her designs and pins them up on her mood board. She likes to take pictures of all her ideas. Emma takes fashion very seriously and she believes that accessories can make or break an outfit. Well, that's what she's always telling her friends!

Inventing adventures

Olivia is a budding inventor. She has her own workshop where she experiments with new ideas and designs amazing gadgets. This summer she has created her most ambitious invention yet—a robot! His name is Zobo.

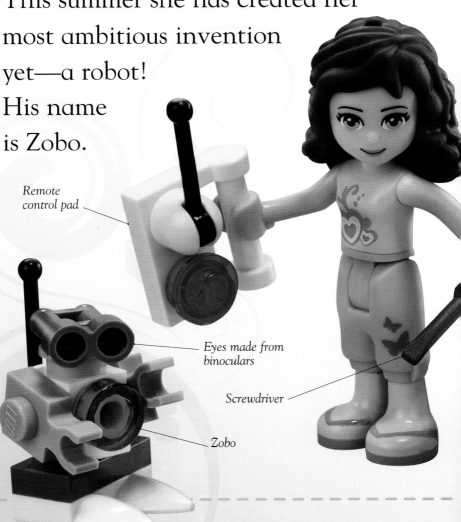

Remote control pad

Eyes made from binoculars

Screwdriver

Zobo

Sometimes Olivia is so busy with her inventions that she forgets to go out and have fun with Emma, Andrea, Mia, and Stephanie.

Olivia thinks Zobo is really cool. She can make him fetch things, using her remote control pad. He is really easy to look after, too. Unlike a pet, he doesn't need walking or feeding, all he needs is regular oiling to make sure he doesn't go rusty.

Oil can

Horsing around

Mia, Emma, and Stephanie all agree that summer is perfect for spending more time with their favorite animals—horses. During the summer Mia spends as much time as possible at the stables, grooming, feeding, and riding her horse, Bella.

Bella

Mia

The riding instructor, Theresa, teaches Emma and Stephanie how to groom horses.

This summer, Stephanie and Emma are going to riding camp, with Stephanie's friend Ella. At riding camp the girls can spend all day with horses. In the morning they have lessons with Theresa, who teaches them how to care for horses.

In the afternoon they can practice riding in the training paddock or go out for longer rides in the countryside. At the end of the day, the girls must groom and feed the horses and then put them safely in their stables.

Helping out

Mia is crazy about all animals, not just horses. During the summer, she is a volunteer helper with the Heartlake City vet. Mia does whatever the vet needs her to. She feeds the animals, cleans their cages, exercises them, and sometimes she just talks to them if they are scared or hurt. Mia loves taking care of animals and they seem to like her, too. She thinks she might like to be a vet one day. Mia knows it is hard work, but she wants to learn as much as possible from Sophie the vet.

Pet transporter

Animal expert

Sophie the vet is Olivia's aunt. She is trained to treat sick and injured pets and wild animals.

Mia

Sophie

Furry friends

During the summer, Andrea and Mia have more free time to spend with their pets. They think that animals need summer adventures, too! Andrea decides that her rabbit deserves star treatment so she builds him a fabulous new living space.

Fresh carrot

Broom

Mia thinks that her puppy, Charlie, needs a summer makeover. She washes and grooms him, and completes the look with a cute pink bow!

The rabbit's new home has an outside area so he can hop around and get plenty of exercise, and an indoor area with a roof so he can stay warm and dry at night. He also has a special water bottle so he will never be thirsty and Andrea makes sure he is well fed with tasty carrots. What a lucky rabbit! He is a very happy bunny.

Makeover time

Emma thinks that Mia's puppy isn't the only one who deserves a makeover. She wants a new look for summer so she goes to the Butterfly Beauty Shop and asks Sarah for something fabulous!

Mirror

Hairdryer

Sarah

Emma is always giving her friends
great fashion advice so Mia is pleased
to be able to help her out, too.

Sarah knows just what to do, and
Emma loves it! Now she just needs to
complete her look with a cute hair
accessory and the perfect shade of
lipstick. Emma can't decide which
lipstick will look best so she needs
advice from one of her friends.
Fortunately, Mia is passing by the
Beauty Shop and is happy to help
Emma out. Her new look is fabulous!

Summer show

Mia has a busy summer, but she makes sure that her pets have fun, too. She enters her puppy, Charlie, into the annual Heartlake City Dog Show. Mia is determined that he will win a prize for Most Agile Puppy, but it is going to take a lot of hard work and practice.

See-saw

Purple bow

Charlie

*Charlie and Scarlett receive winners'
ribbons. They just happen to match their
purple bows perfectly!*

Fortunately, Mia is a talented
animal trainer and Charlie is
very clever. On the day of the
competition he performs brilliantly.
Charlie is the winner! He wins the
special trophy, but Olivia's puppy,
Scarlett, takes second place.

Mia is extremely proud of
her special puppy.

Summer daytrips

Stephanie and Emma love taking trips in their cars. They're happy to drive their friends wherever they want to go—if they can only agree on a plan!

Everyone has a great idea: Emma would like to take a trip to the mall to check out the latest fashions.

Convertible car

Windshield

If Stephanie's friends are too busy to go for a drive, she takes her dog instead!

Mia suggests a drive out to the countryside to go on a nature hike, but Andrea wants to go and see her favorite pop group in concert. Olivia thinks there's a Science Fair in the next town, but Stephanie has heard there might be a soccer tournament at the City Park. Olivia finally comes up with a practical solution: They can do all these things, one at a time! The Science Fair first, of course...

Secret place

Olivia believes that she doesn't have to travel far for the best summer adventures. That's because she and her friends have an amazing treehouse, which no one else knows about. Olivia found the treehouse near her new house when she moved to Heartlake City and the girls worked hard together to fix it up and make it the perfect meeting place. Now it's Olivia, Andrea, Mia, Emma, and Stephanie's own private space.

Telescope
Olivia built a telescope so the girls can check whether anyone is approaching the treehouse.

At the treehouse the girls can hang out, share their secrets, and plan their next adventure.

Mia

Emma

Olivia

Andrea

Stephanie

Amazing adventures

Emma, Stephanie, Mia, Andrea, and Olivia have had lots of fantastic summer adventures—some relaxing, some thrilling, and some downright hard work! However, they all know what the most important part of any summer adventure is—sharing it with your best friends.

Summer is nearly over but the girls have time for one last barbecue at Olivia's house.

Winter adventures

Soon it will be time for some winter adventures. For Emma that means one thing—snow! She loves winter sports, such as skiing.

Friends can make a good summer, a fabulous summer. Now it's your turn: How will you spend your summer adventure? Who will you share it with?

Let's Go Riding!

Written by Catherine Saunders

Animal friends

Olivia, Emma, Stephanie, Mia, and Andrea are best friends and they love hanging out together. The girls have many hobbies, but they share a love of animals.

Stephanie

Puppy

Andrea

Rabbit

The girls care about all animals. However, two of them share a passion for one special type of animal—horses! Come on, let's go riding with horse-crazy Mia and Emma.

Olivia

Bird

Emma

Mia

Hedgehog

Cat

Mia and Bella

Mia is an outdoor girl. She loves camping, canoeing, and riding her horse, Bella. In her spare time, Mia helps the Heartlake City vet care for sick or injured animals.

Mane

Carrot

Beautiful Bella

Bella has a cute white stripe on her head, called a blaze. Mia thinks she's the prettiest horse in the whole world!

Bella

Mia's dream job would definitely involve animals. She might become a vet, an animal psychologist, or work in a pet rescue center.

Hay

Emma and Robin

Emma loves decorating, drawing, and designing clothes. She likes to share her talents with her friends by giving them, or their bedrooms, makeovers.

Emma dreams of becoming a fashion designer or an interior decorator one day.

Emma always seems to know what's in fashion, and what isn't. But there's one thing that will always be in fashion for Emma— her horse Robin. She thinks Robin is simply perfect.

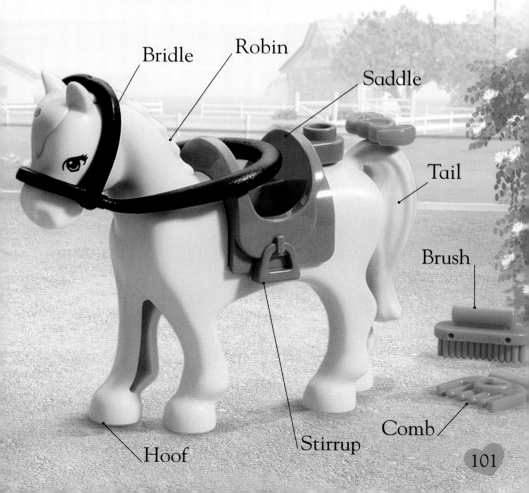

Bridle

Robin

Saddle

Tail

Brush

Hoof

Stirrup

Comb

Horse show

Emma loves horseback riding and her favorite part is jumping. Emma and Robin are a great team and they often enter horse jumping competitions.

Katharina

Gate

Today, Emma and Robin are traveling to a horse show. They plan to win the jumping contest. Emma leads Robin into his blue horse trailer. He travels in style!

Horse trailer

Ramp

Emma is getting Robin ready for the competition. First, she gives him a long drink of water and some carrots so that he has enough energy to jump high over all the fences.

Saddle

Riding hat

Riding boots

Horses love eating carrots. Robin is so gentle and friendly that Emma can feed him carrots straight from her hand.

Bridle

Reins

Next, it's time for Emma to put on her riding hat and boots. Finally, she saddles up Robin. Good luck Emma and Robin!

Emma and Robin have won the competition! Robin cleared all the jumps. Emma is so proud of her clever horse.

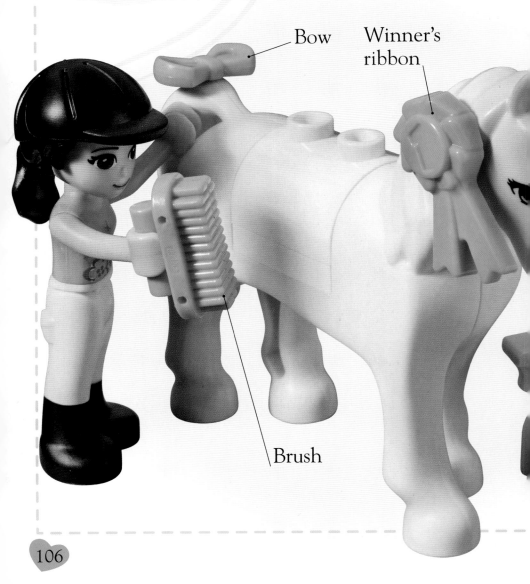

Bow

Winner's ribbon

Brush

Jumping high
Horse jumping is hard. Emma and Robin must time their jump perfectly so they don't knock the fence down.

Emma pins the blue winner's ribbon onto Robin's mane. It's a perfect fashion accessory. Emma cleans and grooms her tired horse. Robin has worked so hard today, but now it's time to go home. Well done Robin, Emma has a special reward for you—some extra carrots!

At the stables

Mia likes to spend as much time as she can with her horse. Every day, after school, she goes to visit Bella at the stables.

Stables

Flag

Horse fan

Katharina would like to be a famous rider or a horse trainer. She has a horse called Niki.

During the school holidays, Mia can spend all day at the stables. Her friend Katharina also likes to spend a lot of time there. Mia sometimes forgets that she needs to hang out with Stephanie, Olivia, Emma, and Andrea too. Stephanie jokes that Mia prefers animals to people!

Mia brushes Bella's mane and tail every day. She also makes sure her horse has plenty of fresh hay to eat.

Looking after a horse isn't simple. Every day, Mia must feed Bella, groom her, and clean out her stable. It's hard work, but horse-loving Mia doesn't mind.

For Mia, the best part of the day is exercising Bella because that means riding her! Mia and Bella often go for very long rides.

They like to practice cantering in the beautiful countryside around Heartlake City.

Tail

Mane

Grass

It's been another busy day looking after their horses, but Mia and Katharina can finally relax. So, how do the two friends like to spend their free time?

Flag

Stable door

Bella

Niki

Mia and Katharina have spent all day with their horses, but they can't wait to come back tomorrow.

They talk about horses and read horse magazines, of course!

Bella and Niki are happy too. They've had a very exciting day thanks to Mia and Katharina.

Now the sleepy horses are safe and secure in their clean stables.

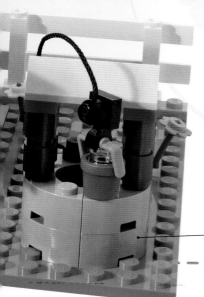

Water well

Off to the vet

Mia is worried about Bella. Something seems to be wrong with one of her front hooves. Poor Bella is limping, but Mia knows someone who can help: Sophie, the Heartlake City vet.

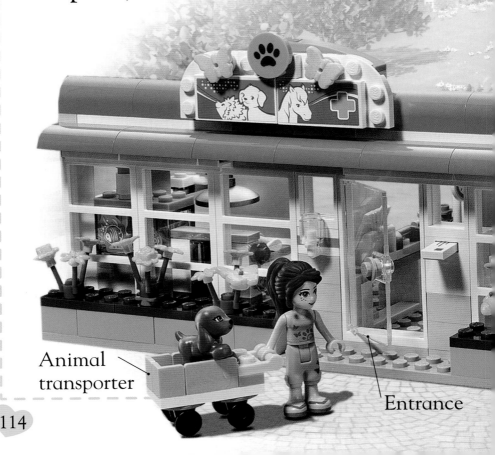

Animal transporter

Entrance

Sophie is also Mia's friend Olivia's aunt. Mia is sure that she'll know exactly what to do for Bella.

Stable

Sophie carefully checks Bella's injured hoof and immediately finds the problem. Bella has a stone in her hoof! The vet very gently removes the stone.

A rescue hedgehog

A sick puppy

Mia loves helping Sophie with the animals. It's good practice for her future career!

Sophie gives Bella a carrot for being such a brave horse. Bella will be fine now, she just needs to rest for a while. So, Mia stays to help Sophie with the other animals, while Bella recovers.

Riding camp

Stephanie also loves horses and she has an idea for the perfect summer vacation—riding camp! She invites Emma and her friend Ella to join her.

Emma and Ella think it's a
wonderful plan. At riding camp
they'll be able to go on long
horseback rides, talk about
horses all day, and make lots of
new, equally horse-crazy, friends.
So, the three excited girls set
off in their stylish minibus.
Riding camp, here they come!

Theresa is an experienced riding instructor and horse expert.

Riding camp is just as much fun as Stephanie, Emma, and Ella thought it would be, but it's hard work too! Theresa, the riding instructor, teaches the girls how to ride horses, how to feed them, and how to care for them.

After their lessons, the girls practice what they have learned in the paddock. By the end of the camp, Stephanie, Emma, and Ella will be expert horse riders!

Robin

Horse cart

Theresa

It's been another fantastic day at riding camp, but Stephanie, Emma, and Ella must go home tomorrow. However, Theresa has something extra-special planned for their last night at camp.

Hot chocolate

Campfire

Marshmallow

Emma and Stephanie are too excited to sleep. They can't wait to tell Andrea, Mia, and Olivia all about riding camp!

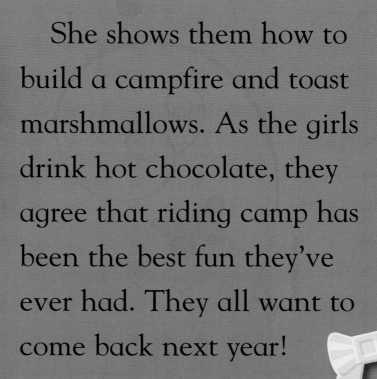

She shows them how to build a campfire and toast marshmallows. As the girls drink hot chocolate, they agree that riding camp has been the best fun they've ever had. They all want to come back next year!

Perfect Pets

Written by Lisa Stock

Welcome to Heartlake City

This is Mia. Do you like animals? Mia does! This is her dog, Charlie.

Charlie sleeps in a cool doghouse that Mia helped decorate.

Mia's friends Olivia, Emma, Stephanie, and Andrea love animals, too. The girls enjoy spending time with all their pets. Let's meet some of them.

Jazz

Jazz is Andrea's rabbit. Andrea grows carrots for her furry friend in her garden.

Carrot

Broom

Jazz makes a big mess eating his carrots! Andrea gets to work tidying the hutch with a broom.

Water

Bucket

Scarlett

Scarlett is Olivia's puppy.
Olivia and Mia train her
to perform in dog shows.
She is great at balancing.

Seesaw

Ball skills

Scarlett wants to improve her soccer skills. She is learning how to weave a soccer ball in between cones. What a great trick!

Doghouse

Bone

Cotton

Stephanie is looking after a newborn lamb named Cotton.

Cotton has gotten very dirty playing outside. Stephanie gently washes her woolly fleece.

Snow
There is another new arrival at Heartlake Stables. Olivia helped deliver a beautiful white foal named Snow.

Brush

Tub

Felix and Max

Felix the cat likes to pounce
and play on the climbing tower
the girls have built for him.

Scratching post

Max the puppy thinks it is much more fun to climb up and down the seesaw outside his playhouse.

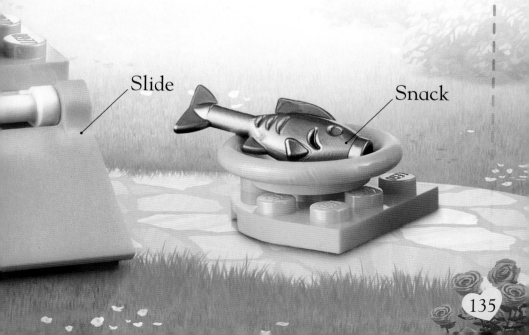

Slide

Snack

Ruby

Ruby is Stephanie's horse. They are entering a jumping competition together.

Bridle

They have been practicing for months! Now Stephanie is sure that Ruby is ready to compete. Good luck, you two!

Saddle

Lady

Lady the poodle is at Heartlake Pet Salon. She loves being washed in the bath and having her hair brushed and trimmed.

Emma

Now Lady is ready to show off her new look on a walk in the park.

Accessories
The salon has so many great accessories, such as bows, clips, and crowns. It's hard to pick just one.

Water dish

Daisy

Daisy is Stephanie's bunny. She has learned how to perform amazing magic tricks with Mia.

Magic wand

Hat

Daisy also helps Stephanie
look for lost animals on a
cool patrol bike.

Playing
cards

Bella

Bella is Mia's horse. Mia makes sure Bella is fit and healthy.

Mia once took Bella to the vet because she had a stone stuck in her hoof. Ouch!

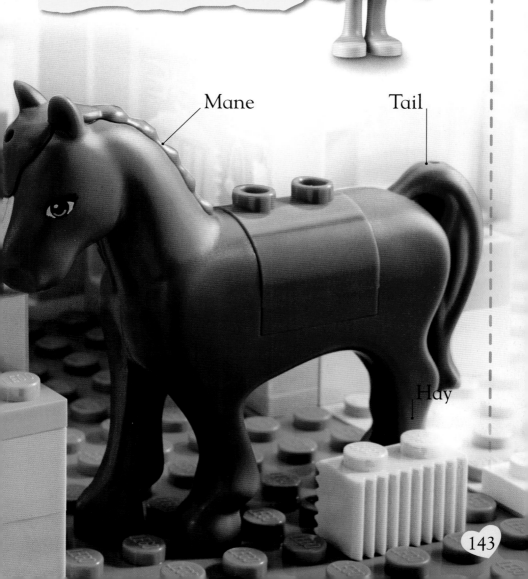

Sophie

Sophie is the Heartlake City vet. The girls take their pets to her for checkups. Sophie makes sure the pets get the help and care they need.

Mane

Tail

Hay

143

On the Ranch

Mia works on her grandparents' ranch with her friend Liza.

Liza

Horses, rabbits, cats, and hens live on Sunshine Ranch, so it is very busy and noisy. The girls have to work hard to keep the place in order.

Cherry tree
This beautiful tree makes the perfect shady spot for the girls to rest in.

Snow

Felix

Jazz

Busy Workers

There are many jobs to do on the ranch. Liza loves feeding carrots to the rabbits.

Liza

Mia collects eggs that
Clara the hen has laid.
The eggs will make
a delicious lunch!

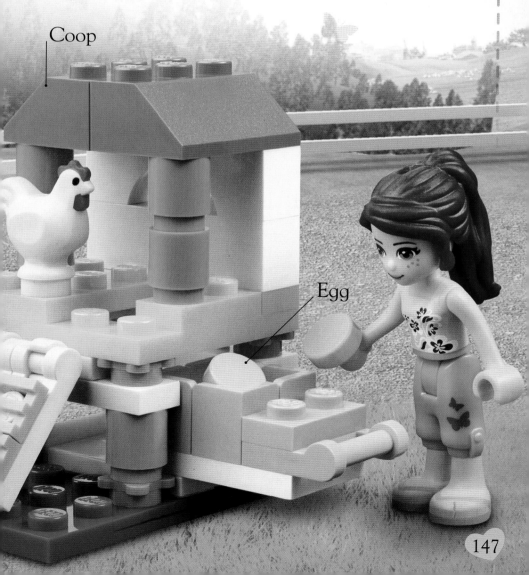

Coop

Egg

Maxie and Goldie

The girls look after Maxie the cat from their club tree house.

The friends also take care of Goldie the bird. When he broke his wing, they built him a beautiful birdhouse to recover in.

Birdhouse